JAMAICA

Ali Brownlie

Photographs by Sue Cunningham

CHERRYTREE BOOKS

Distributed in the United States by
Cherrytree Books
1980 Lookout Drive
North Mankato, MN 56001

Library of Congress Cataloging-in-Publication Data
Brownlie, Alison, 1949-
   Jamaica / by Ali Brownlie ; [photographs by Sue
Cunningham].
      p.cm. -- (Letters from around the world)
   Includes bibliographical references and index.
   ISBN 1-84234-251-7 (alk. paper)
   13-digit ISBN (from 1 January 2007) 978-1-84234-251-0
   1. Jamaica--Social life and customs--Juvenile literature. 2.
Jamaica--Description and travel--Juvenile literature. I.
Cunningham, Susan M. II. Title. III. Series.

F1874.B76 2004
972.92--dc22

                              2004041443

First Edition
9 8 7 6 5 4 3 2 1

First published by
Evans Brothers Ltd
2A Portman Mansions
Chiltern Street
London W1U 6NR

Conceived and produced by

Nutshell
MEDIA

www.nutshellmedialtd.co.uk

Editor: Polly Goodman
Design: Mayer Media Ltd
Cartography: Encompass Graphics Ltd
Artwork: Mayer Media Ltd
Consultants: Jeff Stanfield and Anne Spiring

© Copyright Evans Brothers Limited 2003

All photographs were taken by Sue Cunningham.

Printed in China.

Acknowledgments
The author and photographer would like to thank the Buck
family, the staff and students of Esher Primary School,
Jamaica, and Claudette Salmon for all their help with
this book.

Cover: Travis (second from the right) with his friends
   Davian, Junior, and Jason, in their school uniform.
Title page: Travis (center), Davian and Jason fooling
   about in the sea.
This page: The beach at Negril.
Contents page: Travis and his friends with their catch.
Glossary page: Travis in math class at school.
Further Information page: Playing soccer after school.
Index: Travis covers his friend Jason with sand.

Contents

My Country

Monday, March 5

Green Island
Negril-Montego Bay Road
Jamaica

Dear Sam,

My name is Travis Buck and I'm 9 years old. I live near a small village called Green Island. It's on the island of Jamaica, in the Caribbean Sea. I have two older brothers, Nick and Max, and one younger sister, Whitney. Our grandparents live with us, too. Do you have any brothers or sisters? I can't wait to get a letter from you.

Catch you later!

From

Travis

This is me with my mom, dad, brothers, sister, cousin, and grandma. We're on the veranda of our house. →

Jamaica is the third-largest island in the Caribbean Sea. Only Cuba and Hispaniola are bigger.

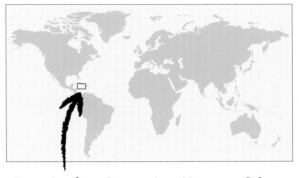

Jamaica's place in the world.

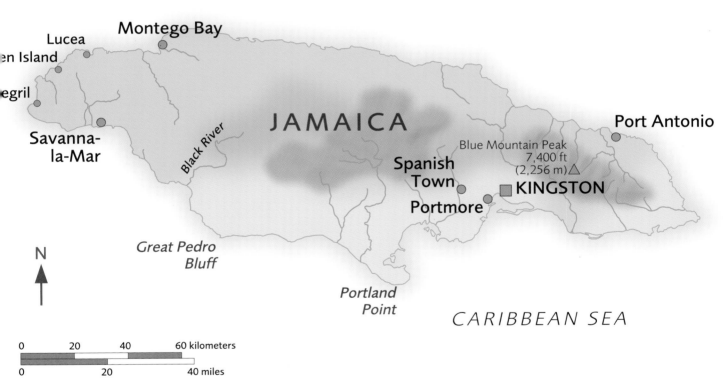

Jamaica was a British colony for about 300 years. It became independent in 1962. Kingston is the capital and also the biggest city.

Green Island is not really an island. It is a small village by the sea, on the west coast of Jamaica. The busy main road between Montego Bay and Negril passes through Green Island.

The beautiful beach at Negril attracts tourists as well as local people.

Negril is a popular beach resort about six miles away from Green Island.
Tourists visit Negril from all over the world.

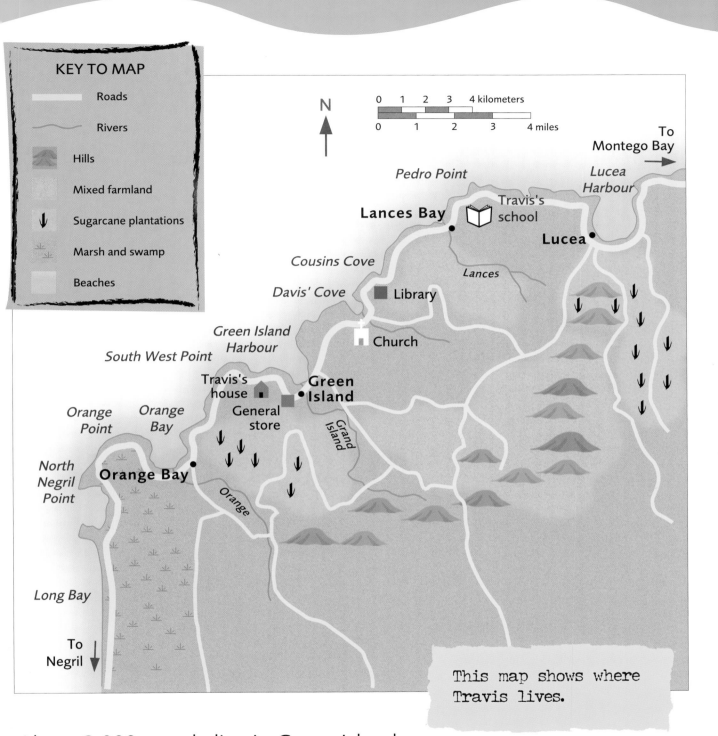

This map shows where Travis lives.

About 2,000 people live in Green Island. There is one general store, a church, and a library. The general store sells most things that people need from day to day. If they need anything special, they have to drive to Montego Bay.

Landscape and Weather

Green Island is surrounded by plantations and other farmland. A short way inland there is a ridge of low hills covered with trees. Many colorful birds, such as hummingbirds, live there.

Jamaica's coastline is lined with golden beaches and rocky shores.

Like the rest of Jamaica, Green Island is hot all year round. Between May and October it can rain heavily in short, sharp bursts. But for the rest of the year, there is very little rain. Sometimes there are hurricanes in September or October.

Tropical fruits such as bananas, mangoes, and breadfruit grow well in Jamaica's hot climate.

Jamaica's Climate

January	July
Temperature	**Temperature**
86 °F (30 °C)	90 °F (32 °C)
Rainfall 1–2 in (46 mm)	**Rainfall** 5–6 in (147 mm)

At Home

Travis's house is made from bricks and concrete. His aunt's house (right) is older. It is made from wood.

Travis's house is on a plot of four houses, where his aunts, uncles, and cousins all live. They spend a lot of time visiting each other's houses.

Ackee is a fruit that grows in Travis's garden. It is part of Jamaica's national dish, ackee and salt fish.

Travis has to water the vegetable patch every day. Beans, tomatoes, and other vegetables grow there.

Travis's house has four bedrooms, a kitchen/living-room, and a bathroom, all on one floor. There is a big garden, where the family grows its own vegetables.

Travis chooses a music
CD to listen to.

Travis likes listening to music on the CD player and watching TV. His favorite music is reggae, which started in Jamaica.

In the evening, the family likes to sit out on the veranda. Most Jamaican houses have a veranda.

Travis shares a bedroom with his brothers. The fan keeps them cool at night.

Wednesday, May 2

Green Island
Negril-Montego Bay Road
Jamaica

Hi Sam,

How's it going? It was hard work here yesterday because our water supply was cut off. Workmen were fixing the road near our house when they hit a water pipe that goes under the road. It's the second time in a month! I had to collect water straight from the pipe and carry it back to the house. We need water for cooking, washing, and drinking so I had to make five trips. Does your water or power ever get cut off?

From

Travis

Collecting the water was hot work but the water kept my feet cool!

Food and Mealtimes

Fried egg and banana for breakfast is a special weekend treat.

Jamaican food includes dishes from other countries. This is because people from all over the world have come to live in Jamaica.

For breakfast, Travis usually has a cup of tea and some fruit. Sometimes he has fried egg or fried banana.

In the evening, the family often eats chicken, rice, and peas cooked in coconut milk. Sometimes they have bammy, which is fried bread eaten with fried fish. On special occasions they have curried goat.

Jerk chicken is a spicy Jamaican dish. It is often sold from stands in the street.

Travis buys lunch from the school cafeteria and eats it outside with his friends. Today it's chicken and rice.

Monday, July 23

Green Island
Negril-Montego Bay Road
Jamaica

Hello there!

Thanks for the recipe you sent me. Here's one for you. It's for Jamaica's national dish — ackee and salt fish.

> You will need: 8 ounces salt fish, 1 can of ackee (look for salt cod and canned ackee in international food stores),
> 3 tablespoons of groundnut oil, 1 large onion, 1 large tomato, 1/2 green chilli (deseeded and chopped), black pepper

In Jamaica we use fresh ackee, but it will be easier for you to buy it in a can.

1. Rinse the salt fish and leave it soaking in water overnight.
2. Chop the onion, tomato, and pepper.
3. Heat the fish in fresh water and simmer for 10 minutes.

The ackee is added to the salt fish.

4. Let the fish cool down and flake it into small pieces with a fork. Make sure there are no bones in it.

5. Heat the oil in a large frying pan (Mom always does that for me.)

6. Fry the onions, pepper, and tomato until the onions are soft.

7. Add the ackee and fish, and cook for another 5 minutes.

8. Add black pepper and serve.

Write and tell me what you think!

From

Travis

The ackee and salt fish are nearly ready. The dish will look a bit like scrambled eggs when it is finished.

School Day

Travis goes to Esher Primary School, which is six miles away. His dad usually drives him there in his taxi. Other children get there by minibus, which they flag down like a taxi. The school day starts with assembly at 8 A.M.

At assembly, all the children line up outside their classroom while their teacher takes attendance.

There are 25 children in Travis's class. Displays of their work are on the classroom walls.

In Jamaica, all children start school at the age of six. When he is 12, Travis will take an exam called the National Assessment Programme. If he passes this he can go to secondary school.

Travis practices writing stories on the computer in the school library.

Travis shows how to do fractions on the blackboard.

Travis's class learns math, English, science, social studies, art, geography, and sport. The school day finishes at 3 P.M., but Travis often stays on after school to play soccer with his friends.

Travis and his friends play soccer on a makeshift field outside the school.

Thursday, August 16

Green Island
Negril-Montego Bay Road
Jamaica

Hey Sam!

I'm glad you liked the recipe I sent you.

Did I tell you about our end-of-term concert? Everyone at school has to put on a performance, either play some music, act in a play, or dance. I belong to a band and we're practicing real hard. We made our drums out of big cans and I played a home-made wooden flute. We'd better win this year.

What do you do at the end of term?

Write soon!

Travis

This is me (on the right) practicing with my band.

Off to Work

In the past, most people from Green Island worked on sugarcane plantations nearby. There are still some plantations, but most of them have closed down. People had to find different jobs.

These miners are off to work at a bauxite mine. Jamaica is one of the world's biggest suppliers of bauxite.

Days on the sugarcane plantations are long, hot, and hard.

Many people from the village now work in hotels and restaurants, in beach resorts like Negril and Montego Bay. Travis's dad is a taxi driver. Many of his customers are tourists.

This woman works in a tourist office. She helps tourists find somewhere to stay and places to visit.

Free Time

Diving from the rocks is great fun. These boys have made sure that the water is deep enough first.

Travis spends every weekend down by the sea. Swimming, diving, and fishing are all favorite sports. He has been on trips to Kingston with his family, but he has never been abroad.

Travis and his friends caught this fish by wading into the sea and grabbing it with their hands.

Saturday, September 8

Green Island
Negril-Montego Bay Road
Jamaica

Hi Sam,

You asked how to play checkers. Here's how we play it:

1. Choose who will have the white counters and who will have the black. Line them up on opposite sides of the board, on the black squares of the back rows.

2. Start by moving one counter at a time. You only play on the black squares, and each counter can only move diagonally.

3. If your counter is next to your opponent's counter, and the square beyond it is free, you can "jump" over it and remove the counter from the board.

4. The winner is the first person to remove all their opponent's counters.

From

Travis

You have to think ahead when playing checkers. ➜

Religion and Festivals

Most people in Jamaica are Christians. There are Rastafarians, Hindus, and Muslims, too. As well as Christmas and Easter, Jamaicans have holidays to celebrate their history and their freedom from slavery.

Churches are usually packed on a Sunday. People join in the service with singing and clapping.

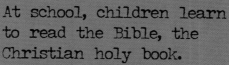

At school, children learn to read the Bible, the Christian holy book.

Jamaicans celebrate Christmas in their own special way. Christmas carols are sung with a reggae beat. There is lots of music and parades, and plenty to eat.

Many children go to Sunday school, where they learn stories from the Bible.

Fact File

Capital City: The capital of Jamaica is Kingston, which has a population of 700,000. Kingston is a major port.

Population: Slightly more than 2.6 million people live in Jamaica.

Size: 4,230 square miles (11,000km²).

Flag: The Jamaican flag has three colors. Black stands for the hardships Jamaican people had to face in the past. Gold stands for the sun. Green stands for the land and hope for the future.

Motto: "Out of many, one." This means out of many different people from all over the world, Jamaica is one nation of people.

Currency: Jamaican dollar. There are 100 cents in a Jamaican dollar.

Main Industries: Tourism, bauxite, sugar, bananas, and coffee.

Language: Jamaica's official language is English, but most people speak Jamaican patois, which is a combination of English, Spanish, Portuguese, and African languages.

Main Religions: Over 80 percent of Jamaicans are Christians. There are also many Rastafarians.

Highest Mountain: Blue Mountain Peak 7,400 feet (2,256 m). Coffee is grown on the slopes of the surrounding mountains.

Longest River: The Black River is 33 miles (53 km) long.

Wildlife: The Black River is famous for its crocodiles. They live to be more than 100 years old. The national bird is the hummingbird. The national flower is the tree of life.

Famous People: Bob Marley was a famous singer, guitarist, and composer of reggae music. He died in 1981 aged just 36. Linford Christie was born in Jamaica in 1960 and went to live in England as a boy. By 1993 he held the World, Olympic, Commonwealth, and European Cup titles for running the 100 meters. Marcus Garvey was born in 1887 and campaigned for freedom for black people, both in Jamaica and in the United States. He died in 1940 and is buried in the National Heroes Park, in Kingston.

Stamps: Jamaican stamps often show famous Jamaican people, such as Bob Marley. Other stamps show wildlife, sports, or scenes in history.

Glossary

ackee A type of fruit that was originally grown in West Africa. It is poisonous if it is not ripe.

bauxite A metal used to make aluminum.

breadfruit A fruit, weighing up to 11 pounds, which is often roasted.

colony A country owned and controlled by another country.

Equator An imaginary line that runs around the middle of the Earth.

hurricane A very severe storm with strong winds and heavy rain.

jerk chicken Chicken that is soaked in spices and barbecued.

plantation A large farm where only one crop is grown.

Rastafarian Someone who follows the Rastafarian religion, a Jamaican religion that began in Ethiopia. Rastafarians are vegetarian.

reggae A type of music that is very popular in Jamaica. It has a heavy, offbeat rhythm.

resort A place where people go on vacation.

salt fish Cod that has been salted and dried to preserve it.

slavery Many of the ancestors of people in Jamaica were brought over from Africa as slaves. They had to work hard for the people who bought them.

sugarcane Tall grass which contains sugar in its sap.

tourism The business of providing services to vacationers.

tropical Between the Tropics of Cancer and Capricorn on the world map. Tropical areas have hot, wet weather all year round.

veranda A porch along the outside of a building. Many houses in hot countries have verandas.

Further Information

Information books:

Brownlie, Ali. *Country Insights: Jamaica*. Chicago: Raintree, 1998.

Brownlie, Ali. *We Come from: Jamaica*. Chicago: Raintree, 1999.

Pluckrose, Henry. *Picture a Country: Jamaica*. London: Franklin Watts, 2001.

McCulloch, Julie. *A World of Recipes: The Caribbean*. Portsmouth, HN: Heinemann, 2001.

Fiction:

Breinburg, Petronella. *Stories from The Caribbean*. Chicago: Raintree, 2000.

Hallworth, Grace. *Sing Me a Story: Song and Dance Stories from the Caribbean*. Atlanta, GA: August House, 2002.

Hanson, Regina. *The Tangerine Tree*. New York: Clarion Books, 1995.

Parker, Victoria. *Traditional Tales from the Caribbean*. London: Chrysalis Books, 2001.

Temple, Francis. *Tiger Soup: An Anansi Story from Jamaica*. New York: Orchard Books, 1998.

Web sites:

CIA Factbook
www.cia.gov/cia/publications/factbook/
Facts and figures about Jamaica and other countries.

Geocities: Caribbean Culture
www.geocities.com/shandycan/culture_notes
An Anansi story.

Jamaicans.com
www.jamaicans.com/childsguide/
A comprehensive children's guide to all things Jamaican.

Jamaica Tourist Board
www.jamaicatravel.com/
Where to go and what to see in Jamaica.

Index